THE NATIONAL POETRY SERIES

The National Poetry Series was established in 1978 to publish five books of poetry every year through participating trade publishers. Publication of the books is funded by James Michener, Edward J. Piszek, The Copernicus Society, The Witter Bynner Foundation for Poetry, Patricia Robinson, The Mobil Foundation, The New York State Council on the Arts, The Ford Foundation, and the five publishers: Random House, Doubleday & Company, E. P. Dutton, Harper & Row, and Holt, Rinehart and Winston.

The National Poetry Series—1984

Wendy Battin, *In the Solar Wind* (Selected by
William Matthews)

Stephen Dobyns, *Black Dog, Red Dog* (Selected by Robert Hass)

Mary Fell, *The Persistence of Memory* (Selected by
Madeline DeFrees)

James Galvin, *God's Mistress* (Selected by Marvin Bell)

Ronald Johnson, *Ark 50* (Selected by Charles Simic)

Black Dog, Red Dog

ALSO BY STEPHEN DOBYNS

POETRY

The Balthus Poems (1982)
Heat Death (1980)
Griffon (1976)
Concurring Beasts (1972)

FICTION

Dancer with One Leg (1983)
Saratoga Swimmer (1981)
Saratoga Longshot (1976)
A Man of Little Evils (1973)

BLACK DOG, RED DOG

POEMS BY

STEPHEN DOBYNS

Holt, Rinehart and Winston / New York *An Owl Book*

Published by Holt, Rinehart and Winston,
383 Madison Avenue, New York, New York 10017.
Published simultaneously in Canada by Holt, Rinehart and
Winston of Canada, Limited.

Library of Congress Cataloging in Publication Data
Dobyns, Stephen, 1941-
Black dog, red dog.
(The National poetry series)
I. Title.   II. Series.
PS3554.02B55 1984   811'.54   83-18611
ISBN 0-03-071077-4

First Edition

Design by Lucy Albanese
Printed in the United States of America
10   9   8   7   6   5   4   3   2   1

Acknowledgments are due to the editors of the following
publications for permission to reprint poems in this book.

Antaeus: "All That Lies Buried," "Art," "The Gun"; *American
Poetry Review*: "Birth Report," "Black Dog, Red Dog," "Caverns of
Darkness," "Chinese Vase," "Dead Baby," "Fight," "Frenchie,"
"Night Swimmer," "North Wind," "The Great Doubters of
History," "This Life," "Under the Green Ceiling," "Wedding,"
"What Did She See?" "Wind Chimes"; *The Black Warrior Review*:
"Dancing in Vacationland"; *Blue Fish*: "Where We Are"; *Crazy
horse*: "Beauty," "Truth"; *Kayak*: "Bleeder," "Kentucky Derby Day,
Belfast, Maine"; *The New Yorker*: "Cuidadores de Autos," "The
Earth from This Distance," "What You Have Come to Expect";
Poetry: "Between Hamburg and Buenos Aires," "General Matthei
Drives Home Through Santiago."

Thanks are also due to the National Endowment of the Arts
for a Fellowship and to the Corporation of Yaddo, which granted
me the time to work on some of these poems.

ISBN 0-03-071077-4

FOR KENNETH ROSEN

Contents

* This symbol is used to indicate a space
between stanzas of a poem wherever
such spaces are lost in pagination.

Black Dog, Red Dog

The Gun

Late afternoon light slices through the dormer window
to your place on the floor next to a stack of comics.
Across from you is a boy who at eleven is three years
older. He is telling you to pull down your pants.
You tell him you don't want to. His mother is out
and you are alone in the house. He has given you a Coke,
let you smoke two of his mother's nonfilter Pall Malls,
and years later you can still picture the red packet
on the dark finish of the phonograph. You stand up
and say you have to go home. You live across the street
and only see him in summer when he returns from school.
As you step around the comics toward the stairs,
the boy gives you a shove, sends you stumbling back.
Wait, he says, I want to show you something.
He goes to a drawer and when he turns around
you see he is holding a small gun by the barrel.
You feel you are breathing glass. You ask if it is
loaded and he says, Sure it is, and you say: Show me.
He removes the clip, takes a bullet from his pocket.
See this, he says, then puts the bullet into the clip,
slides the clip into the butt of the gun with a snap.
The boy sits on the bed and pretends to study the gun.
He has a round fat face and black hair. Take off
your pants, he says. Again you say you have to go home.
He stands up and points the gun at your legs. Slowly,
you unhook your cowboy belt, undo the metal buttons
of your jeans. They slide down past your knees.
Pull down your underwear, he tells you. You tell him
you don't want to. He points the gun at your head.
You crouch on the floor, cover your head with your hands.
You don't want him to see you cry. You feel you are
pulling yourself into yourself and soon you will be

no bigger than a pebble. You think back to the time
you saw a friend's cocker spaniel hit by a car and you
remember how its stomach was split open and you imagine
your face split open and blood and gray stuff escaping.
You have hardly ever thought of dying, seriously dying,
and as you grow more scared you have to go to the bathroom
more and more badly. Before you can stop yourself,
you feel yourself pissing into your underwear.
The boy with the gun sees the spreading pool of urine.
You baby, he shouts, you baby, you're disgusting.
You want to apologize, but the words jumble and
choke in your throat. Get up, the boy shouts.
You drag your pants up over your wet underwear and
run down the stairs. As you slam out of his house,
you know you died up there among the comic books
and football pennants, died as sure as your friend's
cocker spaniel, as sure as if the boy had shot your
face off, shot the very piss out of you. Standing
in the street with urine soaking your pants, you watch
your neighbors pursuing the orderly occupations
of a summer afternoon: mowing a lawn, trimming a hedge.
Where is that sense of the world you woke with
this morning? Now it is smaller. Now it has gone away.

Fight

What was that town on the French coast
at the edge of the Mediterranean? Was it Cassis,
vacation spot of gangsters from Marseilles?
Around it rose hills of sand and scrub pine,
while posted up and down the coast were constant
warnings about forest fires. Even smoking in cars
was forbidden. All day I stopped for hitchhikers
who'd been waiting up to thirty hours for a ride
out of that hot wind. What was that wind called
that blew through Cassis? It was like being crazy,
a burning wind all day and night, whipping sand
in your face, filling your mouth with grit;
and everyone on the street cross and in a hurry,
shopkeepers rude, waitresses on the edge of tears,
cars driving fast and honking their horns.

The three of us walked east along the beach
out of town toward a pine-covered hillside.
At the top was a deserted house with white walls,
a red tile roof and all the windows smashed,
floors littered with trash and broken bottles—
a huge house on a cliff overlooking the sea.
We had meant to sleep there out of the wind
but the house felt too strange, so instead
we chose a slight hollow among the pines
where mosquitoes bit us unmercifully.
Then, past midnight, I noticed a light,
and creeping across the yard to the house,
I saw a flickering candle stuck in a bottle
in one of the downstairs rooms. Standing above it,
two young men were fighting. Both were naked
and their skin shone with sweat as they fought

almost politely, each allowing the other to swing
before swinging himself, or if one fell,
the other would let him get to his feet before
hitting him again—and all of it silent
beneath the roar of wind through the trees.
Someone touched my arm and I turned to find
one of my friends, a Swiss hitchhiker. Frowning,
he motioned me away. They would kill you, he said.

We crept back to our place and I tried to sleep,
but even before sunrise I was up in the gray light.
There was no sign of the two men, no sign of blood
or even the candle, just a swept place on the floor.
I walked back to the cliff and watched the sun
poke its bloody head from the water to my left.
I'd just come from Detroit where I had quit my job
with a newspaper, where I had stopped believing
in a world to be easily measured and described.
I didn't know what might come next but it seemed
the wind, the men fighting and the abandoned house
formed part of it, that together they made up
a mystery which I'd been shown a small piece of.
That morning the sun sent a red streak across
the water to where I sat with my face burning
in a wind that blew all the way from Africa.
In the distance, I saw several small fishing boats
setting out from Cassis. The previous afternoon
I had noticed how their hulls were rusted,
their white paint chipped, but now in the sun's
first light they glistened crimson on the water.
I was just thirty and in my imagination
I put myself on deck staring at the horizon—
that faint line between blue water and blue sky
which from that day forward, or so I lied to myself,
was the only place I could possibly believe in.

Caverns of Darkness

For Ben Tibbs

Dark clouds build to the top of the sky,
while like the undertaker's velvet hand
the air feels heavy with moisture.
Looking from my office window at the midday,
midsummer street, I watch my neighbors
hurriedly do their shopping before the storm.
This one will die of cancer, this one in fire.
This one will be taken in early morning: warmth
draining from him as he sprawls by his sleeping wife.
Now they call to each other, wave greetings
from passing cars. On the curb, a small boy
stabs ants with his thumb. Across the street,
the barber lowers his awning into motionless air.

This morning as dawn broke I was walking
at the outskirts of town. I saw the first light
strike the white clapboard front of the general
store next to the woods, reflect from the silver
chrome of a cash register in the front window.
Waiting at the road's edge, I drew comfort
from that purposeful accumulation of gleaming
vertical and horizontal lines. The sky shifted
from orange to white to dark blue. To the left,
the entangled thicket of chestnut and oak
shaped dark green circles, caverns of darkness.
Through the high grass, I once again saw night
slide into the woods on its obscene white belly.

Birth Report

The week the nuclear protesters stormed the gates
of the Seabrook plant was the same week you were born.
The protesters were repelled. You spent thirty hours
being forced from your mother's body, while I filled
sheets of yellow paper charting the length of each pain.
The week of the first snow was the week you were born.
The week the Pope packed Yankee Stadium. The week of the first
stories of people freezing to death due to the cost of oil.
In bright light, I watched your head ease itself out of
my wife's vagina: your scalp blue, flecked with blood.
The week of the World Series and new trivia on television.
The week politicians maneuvered election year mileage
out of Russian troops in Cuba. The week a racist
from Philadelphia gave me three dollars for your
future and warned you to stay out of Philadelphia.
I took you and bathed you in a plastic tub in the first
seconds of your life, while you twisted and cried; and
outside the world lunged and snapped at the hospital door,
and trees turned color; and corporate business tried
to make certain you would inherit the small change;
and governments arranged a little war for when you got
older; and friends, relatives, even strangers wished you
many fine years on the muckheap, as they pursued their
blindfolded, arms-folded lives and politely helped
each other into the oven. And everybody promised you
your own place in the oven, your own meat hook,
your own hole in the head, own hole in the ground,
as they shut down their brains to the destruction
and stultifying boredom and once more decided
to keep their money on the big promise: the spirit
of this country rising out of the east like a great
red mouth—tearing and rending, devouring its children.

General Matthei Drives Home Through Santiago

The part where General Matthei leaves his office,
I don't know about. And when he gets home,
that I don't know about either. Or if he had
a hard day or an easy day or if his secretary
bent down in front of him so he could see her
large breasts or if he has a secretary or if she has breasts—
all this remains shrouded in mystery. Likewise,
when he got home, whether his four Dobermans
romped out to greet him or if he spent his evening
polishing his pistolas—this too is hidden from me.
But I know for certain it takes twelve men to help
General Matthei drive home; it takes five vehicles:
two motorcycles with sirens and three big gray cars.
Were they Mercedes? They were going too fast to tell.
As for why it is necessary for him to hurry home
so rapidly, this too is a mystery, except
that each day he requires twelve men, five vehicles
and most of the speed in Santiago. It has been said
his bowels were shot away in a duel and the poor general
must spend his life rushing from bathroom to bathroom.
It has been said that as general of the air force
he fears the earth as the wealthy fear the poor.
Or perhaps he is jealous of his wife or has bread
baking in the oven or is accustomed to watching
the American cartoons on the TV at seven-thirty.
But the other generals of the Junta also rush home
at 100 kilometers per hour down the crowded avenidas.
Surely they are not all jealous of their wives.
So again the curtain of mystery is lowered before us.
But yesterday as I was driving home and the general
was driving home and about a million other residents

of Santiago were also going home, I saw the small
humiliation of a middle-aged woman in a small red Fiat
who was neither beautiful, nor was she driving fast.
Maybe she was thinking about her dinner or maybe
her car radio was turned up and she was singing
to the music. In any case, she didn't hear the sirens.
The military policeman riding the first motorcycle
wore white leather gauntlets that nearly reached
his elbows, and when the red Fiat had the audacity
not to scramble for the curb, he swerved around it
and smashed his fist down hard on the red Fiat's hood.
For an instant, that was the loudest noise in Santiago.
Did the red Fiat leap several feet in the air?
I believe it did. Then it braked and swerved right and
dozens of other cars braked and swerved right and blew
their horns and in that moment the general was gone.
I wish I could say all this led to some small tragedy—
that the red Fiat smashed the cart of a man selling bread
or ran over a dog or the woman swallowed her teeth.
But this was a normal evening in late spring and the sky
was as blue as ever and the lowering sun had just begun
to redden the tips of the snow-capped Andes and in another
moment the tangled cars straightened themselves out
and the woman in the red Fiat simply drove home.
When she arrived, maybe she told her husband about
the general and maybe he went out and stared at the Fiat
but saw nothing but a smear in the dust on the red hood.
But maybe he looked at it and the rest of his family
looked at it and maybe he mentioned it to some friends
and they looked at it too. And someday when General Matthei
is shot and dragged by his heels through the streets,
this man will think of his red Fiat and suck his teeth
and, in a way that is typical of the people of Santiago,
he will half roll and half shrug one of his shoulders
as if letting a heavy strap at last slide from it.

All That Lies Buried

Against the streetlight great flakes of snow
look like little sheets of paper tumbling
from the midnight sky. I catch several on my glove,
turn them over—blank on both sides. How
am I to continue with messages like these?
As I walk down the street to the ocean,
I think of all that lies buried by the falling snow:
the pile of firewood that never reached the barn,
last summer's carrots still in the garden.
And those harsh words I said tonight about
separation and the loss of love—I see them now,
little irregular lumps. And whatever hopes
you had, my wife, they're out here too, those cold
unweighables, buried deeper and deeper. And the baby,
our son, who follows us around the house, saying,
Be happy—those words are out here someplace.
It's all out here, every key, knife and coin
I ever lost; every domestic ambition, every little
household improvement I've put back on the shelf.
At the ocean's edge black water laps against
a border of ice. White flakes hit the surface
and disappear. I remember one summer a small bird
with red beak and red eyes running along the surf.
When the water retreated, the bird hurried
to the edge, dug a little, then ran back
as the waves returned. I watched it make its way
down the beach, always working that thin line
between sand and water. Sometimes a wave
rushed in too fast, swamping the bird which
then shook itself and continued, and I liked that,
liked how the bird kept to the very edge.
I even thought, that's the work I want for myself;

as if that line were the division between world
and soul—the place where life itself lies hidden.
But tonight I think, isn't it living at the edge
that makes the trouble—never getting comfortable
or taking anything for granted, never trusting anything?
Across the bay, I see the glimmering of house lights,
no bigger or brighter than stars. Are those the cold
lights of reason or the constant glimmerings of fear?
I feel surrounded by messages I don't understand.
Better to let them go and try forgetting, better
to say there are no messages, that those lights
are no more than people reading or watching the TV.
Tomorrow they'll climb from bed at their usual hour,
trudge off to work and the whole mess will continue.
And me too, I'll climb from bed groggy with sleep
and stand at the window scratching my belly.
Far out to sea I may notice a ship or flashing light.
No telling what it's doing or what it means.
In between will be the huge and rising waves
that beat and beat this poor earth, yet leave
no help, nor guidance, no lesson but confusion.
What does the water leave at the wave's edge?
Whatever it leaves, the waves then hammer it down,
bury it deeper and deeper under the sand, as if
the wave's message, like the message of earth
or snow, is simply burial—the brain's message
to memory, the black dirt's message to a corpse.

Dancing in Vacationland

for Kevin Boyle

The people in the houses behind Searsport are dancing:
the people in tin and tar paper mobile homes, people
in plywood shacks surrounded by junked cars and tires,
broken furniture, hungry geese and chickens, bored
hunting dogs. In ones and twos, they open their doors,
weaving and bobbing out to the road: men in gray
work clothes, women in baggy print dresses; the people
who process chickens, stick fingers down chicken throats
as the chickens come dangling down the line, tearing
out windpipes, tearing out guts; the men and women
who pick meat out of crab bodies, arrange sardines
in little cans; men who work the docks in all weather,
who try to run lobster boats throughout the winter.
These people are now dancing from their houses of
wreckage where they scream at each other and raise
ignorant children and hang on to each other at night.
In threes and fours, they dance toward Searsport and
Route 1. Then, reaching town, they form a single line,
dancing with their arms on their neighbors' shoulders,
dancing in one long row between the shiny antique shops
and fat realtors: one foot up, one foot down, step
to the right, step to the left—lining the highway
which is crowded with tourists from the south
trying to soak up picturesque views of the ocean.
But this morning all they can see are people dancing,
these bloated potato-fed people dancing, these people
who live by collecting returnable bottles, by picking
over the trash at the dump, by trading their bodies,
their wits, their health for a few dollars
and a shack behind Searsport. This morning, because
it is warm and sunny and because they just can't

stand it anymore, they decided to start dancing:
one foot up, one foot down. And the tourists from New York
stop their cars and the tourists from Massachusetts
take pictures and the tourists from Connecticut
feed candy to the little ones, until at last the realtors
and tour guide directors and lobster shack owners,
until at last the alternative life-style farmers,
gift-shop operators, local chamber of commerce,
town police, state police and sheriff's department
all band together and a spokesperson apologizes
to the tourists from the south and begs them
to take no more pictures; and they try to make
the people stop dancing, but the people won't listen
and keep right on dancing—one foot up, one foot down—
so they push them back off Route 1, push them back
to the little roads behind Searsport, push them back
into the tin and tar paper mobile homes, the plywood
shacks surrounded by junked cars, but through the windows
they can still be seen dancing, dancing into the night
in their little paper houses, until at last they lie down
and hold on to each other, hang on to each other
as if afraid of sinking into the earth, afraid the whole
vacationland world might stop spinning beneath them.

What Did She See?

We had come to the English Hospital in Tangier
and my friend kept screaming none of the needles
were clean. He was drunk, had a bad toothache
and in general it had been one of those evenings.
Novocain would soothe him but he wanted
to see the doctor's credentials. I pretended
not to know him. Then a woman took my arm,
asked if I would help her. She was an American
living in Málaga who had come over to Morocco
for the day with a friend, a man in his fifties,
whom she had known just a short time. Although
attractive, she must have been fifty herself.
They had been in a hotel room making love
when suddenly the man lifted his head and died,
right there on top of her, still inside her.
She had lain quietly for a moment before heaving
him off, lain half in passion, half in horror.
Now there was a question of passports and identity;
she needed to get home, had to be in Geneva
on Wednesday, hardly knew this man who had
died on top of her, wouldn't be able to stay
for the funeral, had no idea about next of kin
or if the man had a family, friends who would
claim him, bury him in a way that was proper.
My friend kept shouting at the Moroccan doctors,
shouting in a German accent so they wouldn't know
he was American—not because he thought himself
a discredit to his country, but just the opposite.
The Vietnam War was still dragging on
and he thought his country a discredit to him.
As for the woman, I called the consulate, then
sat with her until someone came. She had been

all prepared for a little holiday, a little
diversion from her expatriate's life in Málaga.
If asked, she could describe the exact curve
of her life with the luncheons marked in advance,
the trips to Paris, the wrinkles all ironed out.
As when you are driving along a winter road
and your car hits some ice, slides out of control—
so had this woman's life taken such a turn.
As for the man, I found myself speculating
what he had thought or if he had time to
think at all, if his death had appeared first
as orgasm, beauty become terror, as Rilke says.

Anyway, I chose to stay with my friend whose comedy
unwound itself out of the hospital to a Moroccan
dentist, whom our cabdriver coaxed from bed
at three in the morning. Strapped to a barber chair,
my friend shouted, Fuck Nixon, fuck Nixon, to wipe out
the pain as his wife and the dentist, as even
the cabdriver and myself stared into his mouth.
Oh, what a pink mouth it was and think of the pain
it held there. We leaned over his chair, almost
pushing each other out of the way to see into
that quivering pinkness, like an animal turned
inside out, or a rabbit once it's been skinned.
We stood looking into that scream as if looking
into the world where everything goes wrong,
where suddenly you are making love to a corpse,
where your car plunges into a ditch, where
the hippie vacation breaks apart on rotten teeth;
looking into that pink hole as if looking
for some way to do it differently or for some
early warning, but there is nothing, nothing at all.
And later, back at our dingy hotel, and my friend
knocked out on pills, and me sleeping, suddenly
I'm waked up by his wife screaming in the hall.

I hit the door, flick on the light and all around
the gallery, people are poking their heads
from their rooms or peering over the balcony
or looking up from the downstairs hall at this
pretty American girl in her nightgown screaming.
What is it? What did she see? Nothing, nothing.
For a second the world snapped up her attention
before rolling off in one more awful black circle.

It Does No Good

Certainly he looks foolish, even preposterous—
a middle-aged man in a ragged sportcoat
surrounded by furniture at a stoplight,
a pile of rugs, chairs, lamps on the sidewalk.

When the light changes and cars come to a halt,
the man holds up a chair and shouts, *Sillas*,
or chairs, offering them for sale. Then the light
turns green and the crowd of cars roars off.

Certainly on every street in Santiago people
sell merchandise at stoplights—toothpaste,
soap, toolboxes, towels, extension cords.
The newspaper even jokes about it: that the way

to boost the economy is to put up more stoplights.
But the man selling chairs sells his own chairs.
He wears a striped tie and his white shirt is clean.
He's not drunk, and his embarrassed laugh, almost

a giggle, proves that he knows he is doing
something absurd. It is a warm sunny day
in early fall, and the smell of burning leaves
mixes with the exhaust fumes. How long did it

take him to come to this? How long did he
look for a job? How long did he borrow money?
I stand across the street and watch. No one
will buy anything. He's too crazy. Besides,

how can you stop your car in heavy traffic
to bargain over a rug? At first, the man's
hair was neatly combed. He's thin but doesn't
look starving. When did he make up his mind?
*

16

Even his wife must have thought he was crazy.
And his kids, they must have snuck from the house
early this morning completely humiliated. Can you
imagine watching your old man hawking the tables

and TV to Hondas and Renaults? There's no
humor in his eyes, no laughing. They look
stretched and dart from driver to driver. No one
looks back, just some boys across the street

and me, standing in front of a butcher shop.
A man's house is an extension of himself. He
must have woken up this morning with the plan
already fixed in his head. It probably took

six trips to bring that stuff to the stoplight.
He must have worried something might be stolen.
He must have known that any friends, relatives,
any family would think him ridiculous. All those

tables and chairs can't be worth fifty bucks
and now he'll have to carry them back again.
Why doesn't he do something violent like smash
the furniture, throw the lamps at passing cars?

But he does nothing, simply stands with a small
chair raised above his head and grins. He no longer
even shouts, *Sillas*, but just stands. What foolish
thoughts run like white mice through his brain?

It does no good to be crazy if you're poor—
no money for cigarettes, no money for shoes,
no money for razor blades, a can of tuna fish,
beer, whiskey, no money to buy a tin cup.

Under the Green Ceiling

Two men walk along the edge of a country road.
One is joking and talking about girls, describing
the abrupt curve from waist to buttocks and how
it sometimes seems the whole world lives there.
As he talks, he idly tosses rocks into the field
on his right, a field of purple clover spotted
with yellow flowers. The rocks clip the flowers or
green leaves, then disappear into the darkness beneath.
It is a cloudless afternoon in midsummer
and in the distance a green locomotive drags
a string of red boxcars toward the horizon.

The other man has hardly eaten for two days.
He is silent and has almost made up his mind
that when they reach the shelter of the woods
half a mile distant, he will rob his companion,
whom he met only that morning. He has a knife
and intends only to show it, but if the other man
wants to fight, well, so much the worse for him.
And he imagines how the knife will slide up
under the ribs, how he'll drag the body off the road,
then escape over the field to the railway line.
So, while the one man talks about girls,
the other tries to steel himself and feel hatred
for his companion, tries to make him the focus
for all that has gone wrong in his life—
the loss of his job, desertion of his family.

Shortly, the man talking about girls begins
to think of his wife, whom he hasn't seen
for nearly a month. And partly he talks
to keep from thinking about her and partly

to keep her a teasing question in his mind.
Will she still love him? Has she found someone else?
He thinks of times they made love when he would
sit back on his haunches straddling her ankles
and see how her body was spread out beneath him;
and as he talks the memory of his wife naked
upon the bed fills his mind, while the rocks he
tosses into the field become the fears of betrayal
and desertion that he one by one pushes from him.

Days later the other man is arrested in the city
and as he awaits the slow unfolding of justice
he tells himself how foolish his companion
had been with his constant talk about girls
and how he deserved all that had happened.
He has no sense of himself as a fragment.
He has no sense of how he and his dead companion
made up one man. Add a third and he's still
one man; add a fourth, likewise. But by himself,
he's a fragment of wall, part of a broken pot;
he's like the quivering rodent under its
protection of leaves, terrified when the chance
rock crashes through its green ceiling, victim
of a world that is endlessly random and violent.

Wind Chimes

Begin with a Victorian cottage in a Rhode Island
resort town—a two-story house of yellow shingles
a block from the ocean with a roof like a Chinese
pagoda and a screened-in porch on three sides.
A wooden croquet set lies scattered on the lawn
which is surrounded by a chest-high privet hedge.
Hanging from the porch ceiling, a wind chimes
with eight glass bars swings gently in a breeze
smelling of salt and fried food from hot dog stands
along the beach. In the middle of the living room,
a boy lies on his stomach reading a Batman comic.
Around him are wicker chairs with white cushions.
The boy's knees are bent and the soles of his tattered
gym shoes point toward the ceiling. As he reads,
he slowly bumps his heels together as if in time
to the sound of the surf he hears in the distance.
A collie dog lies panting at the foot of the stairs,
while in a bedroom at the top of the stairs
a man lies naked on white sheets smoking a cigarette.
His wife, also naked, sleeps with her head on his chest.
As he smokes, the man carelessly strokes her back and
stares up at the lines and angles of the white ceiling
until it seems he's looking down from some high place,
a plane or hilltop. From where he lies, he can just see
the roofs of other houses and he imagines his neighbors
drowsing their way through the August afternoon.
White curtains sway in the breeze from the open window,
while the smoke from his cigarette seems to turn blue
as it rises through bars of sunlight to the ceiling.
From nearby, the man hears the sound of people
playing tennis—an occasional shout and the plonk
of the ball against the webbing of the racket;
from the porch, he hears the tinkling of wind chimes
like a miniature orchestra forever warming up.
*

20

Years later the same man is lying fully clothed
on his bed in a city hotel. It is evening and
the only light comes from the street and a blinking
red sign outside his window. He's waiting for a friend
and soon they will go to dinner, but as he waits
he watches the shadows on the ceiling and either that
reminds him of the wind chimes or perhaps
it is some combination of sounds from the street.
His son is grown up; his wife has remarried.
He himself has a new wife in another city
and he's away from home only because of his work
in which he thinks himself happy and successful.
But for a moment, he clearly hears the wind chimes,
sees the swaying curtains in that summer bedroom,
even feels the faint pressure of his ex-wife's
sleeping head upon his chest. But then
it slips by and in its place he has an awareness
of all the complicated turnings of his life,
and he wonders if what he had seen as progress
was only a scrambling after circumstance, like a boy
trying to scramble into the back of a moving truck;
and while he doesn't regret his life, he grieves
for all that was lost, all that he had to let go.
He thinks of that ocean house and wishes he were back
in his former life or that one could take one moment
and remain inside it like an egg inside its shell,
instead of constantly being hurried into the future
by good luck or bad. Again he hears the wind chimes,
even sees them hanging in the dark with their
eight glass bars and red oriental designs, but then
they begin to get smaller as if quickly receding,
until they are no more than a speck of bright light
which at last blinks out as his friend starts hammering
at the door and his whole busy life rushes forward.

Wedding

It was either summer or a hot day
in late spring. We had taken a five o'clock
commuter train to a Chicago suburb
where a friend was being married—an ugly
yellow train with two levels of plastic seats
and the windows all filthy. It was crowded
with office workers reading newspapers
or sheafs of notes taken from briefcases.
Everybody was sweating like crazy.
We had nursed our friend through high school
and into college, had seen him through late nights
of drinking and speeding cars. I say we, but
mostly it was you, since I had little patience
with those four A.M. discussions where you
talked him out of every form of self-destruction.
He had appeared too frail, a sheet of glass
too thin for any of the windows he seemed
destined for, yet here he was nearly married
and preparing to go out and teach school.
The train stopped abruptly in a field littered with
empty barrels, junked cars, piles of rusted metal.
For half an hour we sat in the increasing heat—
a landscape of gray corrugated buildings, hazy sky.
Then at last an ambulance bumped down the service road
and two men hurried into the train with a stretcher.
Five minutes later, they emerged—a red blanket
completely covering whatever they were carrying,
while behind them came a conductor holding
a hat and briefcase. The men slid the stretcher
into the ambulance, tossed in the briefcase
and took the hat from the conductor who had been
dusting it off on his sleeve. Minutes later

we were on our way, everybody nervously talking
and sweating worse than ever. You crossed yourself
and I kept thinking of the man who certainly
had had plans for that evening, and the people,
probably a wife and family, who were someplace still
expecting him. We were nearly late to the wedding.
The organist was playing versions of popular songs.
Our friend was quickly married and we had
the sense of his falling from our hands and care
into someone else's. Years later I heard
how he was a popular teacher, that he was even
intending to run for some town office,
and it seemed he had successfully cleared
the ditch of unhappy adolescence into a career
of community service—some stuff like that;
but at least he had come to endure his life.
Why does this come back to me today? Since dawn
it's been raining, turning the old snow to mush,
turning the ocean into a vast gray blur.
I think of you now in another state, coping
with your life, and your eyes which despite doctors
and operations steadily fail you year by year;
but surrounded by your husband and friends
who love you. I remember how you watched
the attendants carrying the man on the stretcher
who seemed almost delicate under his red blanket,
although any need or fear of delicacy was past.
I remember how you lowered your head, turning away.
Lucky bastard, at least he's out of it, you said.
And then the train lurched once and dragged us forward.

The Earth from This Distance

The man on skis at the edge of the forest
glides forward through powdery snow. Among
the trees to his left, he feels the presence
of his vanity and anger, bitterness toward the
world and himself, envy and those hateful grudges.
He pictures them loping along in the half dark
cursing and muttering to themselves as he
pushes himself forward under a cloudless sky.
He imagines stumbling and the whole clumsy lot
hopping and squeaking toward him, flinging
their soft bodies against him, until he
begins to ski faster just to escape them.
In the world too he finds himself hurrying faster
as he tries to deal with people's expectations,
ambition, the constant demands of money,
until he wants to give it up, quit the whole mess.
As he thinks this, his left ski dislodges a mouse
from the snow which pops up, tries to scurry
across the surface to the woods. Just as the mouse
has nearly reached the shelter of the pines, a hawk
drops from a branch, snatches the mouse and flaps
upward with the mouse dangling apparently unhurt
from the hawk's precise talons. The man stops.
He cannot think where he is going. He watches
the hawk dwindle to a brown speck in the blue sky
and imagines he's been given a sign, but feels
too stupid to understand. He is endlessly sick
of this self-absorption, of inhabiting a quarrel.
Where was the hawk in his own life? Why can't he
heave from himself this blanket of self-complaint?
Slowly the man skis forward. He tries to conceive of
the mouse's terror as it was struck by the hawk

but instead feels a mixture of freedom and release,
as if the world might rid him of the need to choose.
He imagines the great talons battening onto his shoulders,
plucking him from the ground like a single grape
from a white plate, lifting him higher and higher,
until the snowy hills appear as a flat surface
with the trees so many black marks upon it—
like a page with the letters all jumbled
and no hope to make sense of it in this life.

Where We Are

After Bede

A man tears a chunk of bread off the brown loaf,
then wipes the gravy from his plate. Around him
at the long table, friends fill their mouths
with duck and roast pork, fill their cups from
pitchers of wine. Hearing a high twittering, the man

looks to see a bird—black with a white patch
beneath its beak—flying the length of the hall,
having flown in by a window over the door. As straight
as a taut string, the bird flies beneath the roofbeams,
as firelight flings its shadow against the ceiling.

The man pauses—one hand holds the bread, the other
rests upon the table—and watches the bird, perhaps
a swift, fly toward a window at the far end of the room.
He begins to point it out to his friends, but one is
telling hunting stories, as another describes the best way

to butcher a pig. The man shoves the bread in his mouth,
then slaps his hand down hard on the thigh of the woman
seated beside him, squeezes his fingers to feel the firm
muscles and tendons beneath the fabric of her dress.
A huge dog snores on the stone hearth by the fire.

From the window comes the clicking of pine needles
blown against the glass by an October wind. A half moon
hurries along behind scattered clouds, while the forest
of black spruce and bare maple and birch surrounds
the long hall the way a single rock can be surrounded

by a river. This is where we are in history—to think
the table will remain full; to think the forest will

remain where we have pushed it; to think our bubble of good fortune will save us from the night—a bird flies in from the dark, flits across a lighted hall and disappears.

North Wind

As you climb the hill, you dig your heels into new snow,
trying to miss patches of ice so you won't slide back.
With a length of ice-covered rope, you drag your sled,
a Flexible Flyer, behind you. It is nearly dark and
you are alone on the hill. Even your dog has gone home.
You think of her in your warm kitchen, watching
your mother make dinner as your younger brother
plays with his blocks under the kitchen table.
Here on the hill it has again begun to snow.
Reaching the top, you scoop powdered snow into your
blue mitten, press it against your mouth; then you
turn your sled, position it at the crest of the hill.
To your left are the lighted houses of your neighbors,
the darkening expanse of white backyards; to your right
a gray mass of trees. Using your fists as oars, you push off.
Snowflakes sting your face as you gather speed, rush down
the bank barely avoiding fence posts, apple tree, black bush.

In your favorite book, *At the Back of the North Wind*,
the woman who is the north wind often comes at night
for the boy Diamond and bears him up into the dark sky.
High in the air there's a place where you believe he leaves
his old life, becomes part of the life of the north wind,
who loves him. All afternoon you think if you can just make
your sled hurtle fast enough down the slope, then you too
will pass through the ice heart of the north wind, cross
this line at the edge of your life, which even at eight
feels much too complicated to reach a place of contentment.
Not until years later do you realize this hairline
you tried to sled across was the line of your own death,
that by going fast enough you could sled out of your life,
become swallowed up in whiteness and cross through
to a green world without punishment or disappointment.
*

When you reach the bottom, the sled swerves toward the trees
and you fall off. Although it is now dark, you decide
the track is much slicker and you will try one last run.
Climbing back, you hear your mother whistling you home
to dinner, but you only go faster, climbing on all fours.
Near the top, you pick up your sled, carry it to the crest.
The only light comes from the back windows of houses,
forming a patchwork of light and dark on the hillside.
Raising the sled, you turn and run down the hill and
when you can run no faster you fling yourself forward,
crying out as the air is knocked from your lungs,
barely hanging on as you fly down the hill so rapidly
you nearly don't see the apple tree when you pass within
inches of its trunk. But this time, even as the snow fills
your eyes, you see a brightening as if the back windows
were joining into one great light, and you think
you see the woman with white, white skin and endless
black hair who will lift you gently from your sled,
wrap you in the folds of her glacier-green robe.

As the sled gains speed, hurtling over the rough surface,
you stretch out your hands toward the increasing light
and woman with clouds of black hair. But instead of
careening across the border of your life, the sled
flies up over a stump, a buried log, a hidden rock
and you fly head over feet in the opposite direction,
fall back to a world that chafes like the frozen ground
you skid across. When you come to a stop, you lie
staring up at black sky and stray white flakes. Then you
seek out your sled and limp home. So what has happened?
Do you still think this earth a place to be escaped from,
that you can become wind, nothing but wind? Now the earth
grips your ankles with two greedy hands, and each year
it pulls you deeper into its body till at last you take
your place in the adult world: standing like tall grass
in an angry field, grass that lashes and buffets itself
where there is no wind, no least kiss of air.

Bleeder

By now I bet he's dead which suits me fine,
but twenty-five years ago when we were both
fifteen and he was camper and I counselor
in a straightlaced Pennsylvania summer camp
for crippled and retarded kids, I'd watch

him sit all day by himself on a hill. No trees
or sharp stones: he wasn't safe to be around.
The slightest bruise and all his blood would simply
drain away. It drove us crazy—first
to protect him, then to see it happen. I

would hang around him, picturing a knife
or pointed stick, wondering how small a cut
you'd have to make, then see the expectant face
of another boy watching me, and we each knew
how much the other would like to see him bleed.

He made us want to hurt him so much we hurt
ourselves instead: sliced fingers in craft class,
busted noses in baseball, then joined at last
into mass wrestling matches beneath his hill,
a tangle of crutches and braces, hammering at

each other to keep from harming him. I'd look up
from slamming a kid in the gut and see him watching
with the empty blue eyes of children in sentimental
paintings, and hope to see him frown or grin,
but there was nothing: as if he had already died.

Then, after a week, they sent him home. Too much
responsibility, the director said.

Hell, I bet the kid had skin like leather.
Even so, I'd lie in bed at night and think
of busting into his room with a sharp stick, lash

and break the space around his rose-petal flesh,
while campers in bunks around me tossed and dreamt
of poking and bashing the bleeder until he
was left as flat as a punctured water balloon,
which is why the director sent him home. For what

is virtue but the lack of strong temptation;
better to leave us with our lie of being good.
Did he know this? Sitting on his private hill,
watching us smash each other with crutches and canes,
was this his pleasure; to make us cringe beneath

our wish to do him damage? But then who cared?
We were the living children, he the ghost
and what he gave us was a sense of being bad
together. He took us from our private spite
and offered our bullying a common cause:

which is why we missed him, even though we wished
him harm. When he went, we lost our shared meanness
and each of us was left to snarl his way
into a separate future, eager to discover
some new loser to link us in frailty again.

Funny

These guys, it's hard to believe these guys.
They're stuck in a halfway house for half crazy vets
at the top of the hill and they stroll through town
with their hands in their pockets or waving at cars.

Or you see them in bars eating an ice cream cone
or maybe drinking beer, although with all that
medication you'd think they couldn't drink, but
what the heck they've probably got lobotomies. Anyway

they'll sit in a bar like Curly, Moe and Shemp
grinning and staring at the girls, I mean, any
girls or sometimes they'll just focus on a blank
spot on the wall or a flickering Budweiser sign.

One time one of them crept up behind the city
council president who was sipping a martini
and he's got orange hair like a dandelion clock
and this crazy vet just ruffled it like you might

rub down a watermelon or feel a tit. The guy from
the council swore he'd never seen the vet before,
although you wonder how he ever missed him, and he
would have decked him if the vet hadn't left so quick.

They all wear funny hats to either warm their brains
or keep their heads from popping off, you don't know which.
And they look like teenagers somehow, although they're
pushing fifty. One of them keeps his graying hair

in a perfect duck's ass haircut, wears a jacket with
padded shoulders and makes wolf whistles at girls.

I keep picturing him in Korea on Hill 366
like in that movie with Gregory Peck, and the Chinese

keep shelling them all day and night and each shell
clicks his life another notch toward Belfast, Maine.
And this guy, he's probably from Nebraska or someplace
and he quit high school in 1951 and took a job

in a garage so he can work on his car, a 1948
purple Merc with a chopped top so the windshield's
only six inches high and double chrome pipes and
huge chrome bumpers, and I think of this guy

trying to peer into that chrome, because in his head
it's still 1951 even though he's sitting in the Belfast
Cafe with an ice cream cone, and he's searching
for his face in the chrome, but it's distorted

like in a trick mirror, and he can't see it's him,
can't see it's his old motorcycle cap, his DA haircut,
his scarred forehead, his wandering and witless
fifty-year-old eyes. Now that's what I call funny.

Spring Rain

Drill holes in small rocks, then press your lips
to each hole and blow. One by one the rocks
get bigger, edges sharper. This is what I've
got in my stomach that the dopes call anger.
Just writing it makes me want to smack my face,
break this pen. The same dopes will all tell you
a thing of beauty is a joy forever, well I guess
that lets me out. Let me explain what I mean:
not long ago in Spain I stood on a cliff above
the city of Jaén, above the gray of its cathedral,
the pink stone high rises thrown up for workers.
It'd been raining all morning and gray sky reached out
hundreds of miles over the abused red clay land
where every fifteen feet grew another olive tree:
millions of trees with twisted dark trunks and
wet leaves pointing in millions of directions
like nervousness or love in a flutter. My anger
was with me then in the rain and I wanted to
chip and chisel it free from my body, leave it
like a heavy stone at the bottom of deep water.
I wanted to drift out above that olive-covered land
until my body broke apart like cloud or spring rain.
Two feet stuck in angry dirt is no way to do a life.
Far below me houses hunkered down like warts on a hand,
as narrow streets twisted and intersected: turning,
turning back on themselves, always back on themselves.

Back

Patterns of the invisible: white branches
against whiter snow—what house is this
with its windows broken, its door torn
from its hinges? Standing in the doorway,
I see how the wind has covered the floor,
the tipped-over chairs and broken table
with a thin layer of snow, covered
the room like a rumpled sheet over a bed.
Outside, a cardinal hops from branch to branch
in the late afternoon sun—its splash
of scarlet seems the landscape's one color.
I recall this house in summer and the woman
who lived here, even her simplest gesture—
how her hands held a book, peeled an orange,
arranged blue flowers in a yellow bowl.
Always to order one's life around some
future event, never to value the present—
this is how the future is lost.
I call out: I am back, I am back.
A breeze from the window lifts a spiral
of snow, sends it dancing and skittering
across the floor until I lose it
in the blank whiteness of the room—patterns
of the invisible: white branches, whiter snow.

This Life

"Maestro, chi son quelle genti che
l'aura nera si gastiga?"
—Canto V, *The Inferno*

Blue sky to the south, clouds to the north,
racing tatters of cloud in between—although
here only the first flakes have begun to fall,
in the distance the mountains are tugging on
their winter caps. Outside, a spiral of snow
whirls between window and forest's edge
like a man fighting his way out of a sheet.
Inside, this is a college class on translation.
The teacher recites the line: "'I love
this poor earth because I know no other.'
Is it earth or country? What difference
does this make?"
                           Once more I think of you
six thousand miles south in your poor country,
and again I count all the possible reasons
why I haven't heard from you—bad mail,
bad politics, bad love. I think of how Dante
condemned his lovers to an existence of wind
and try to imagine us brought together
in the frantic white spiral that rushes between
the window and winter trees. To be so joined to you—
the thought brings my heart to my throat.
But without you—that's me out there alone.
Blue sky to the south, clouds to the north—
in another hour when this class is over
and the wall of cloud has reached the horizon,
the spiral of snow will have vanished: lost
in that falling white blanket, this life,
which as we return to our separate rooms
we will say is so impossible to walk through.

Leaving Winter

From the backyard next door comes the sound
of a woman's laugh, deep in her chest and rolling
like the sound of barrels rolling down the street.
As I guess at her pleasure, the laugh gets deeper.

From where I sit on the back steps, the white walls
of the backyard seem to encage the warm spring air
the way a small wicker box can hold a songbird.
A lemon tree next door hands its fruit over the wall.

And rising high over the wall, the fifty-foot Virgin
perched atop San Cristobal Hill with arms outstretched
seems to be inviting small planes to dance. Oh,
propeller of pleasure, soft featherbed of blue sky.

I feel a pressure in my stomach and chest and seem
unable to catch my breath. I ask myself, What new
pain is this? Then I realize I am happy. Behind me
out of winter, footsteps wind through dirty snow.

Black Dog, Red Dog

The boy waits on the top step, his hand on the door
to the screen porch. A green bike lies in the grass,
saddlebags stuffed with folded newspapers. The street
is lined with maples in full green of summer, white houses
set back from the road. The man whom the boy has come
to collect from shuffles onto the porch. As is his custom,
he wears a gray dress with flowers. Long gray hair
covers his shoulders, catches in a week's growth of beard.
The boy opens the door and glancing down he sees yellow
streaks of urine running down the man's legs, snaking
into the gray socks and loafers. For a year, the boy
has delivered the man's papers, mowed and raked his lawn.
He's even been inside the house which stinks of excrement
and garbage, with forgotten bags of groceries on tables:
rotten fruit, moldy bread, packages of unopened hamburger.
He would wait in the hall as the man counted out pennies
from a paper bag, adding five extra out of kindness.
The boy thinks of when the man's mother was alive.
He would sneak up to the house when the music began
and watch the man and his mother dance cheek to cheek
around the kitchen, slowly, hesitantly, as if each
thought the other could break as simply as a china plate.
The mother had been dead a week when a neighbor found her
and even then her son wouldn't let her go. The boy sat
on the curb watching the man hurl his fat body against
the immaculate state troopers who tried not to touch him
but only keep him from where men from the funeral home
carried out his mother wrapped in red blankets, smelling
like hamburger left for weeks on the umbrella stand.

Today as the boy waits on the top step watching the urine
trickle into the man's socks, he raises his head to see

the pale blue eyes fixed upon him with their wrinkles and
bags and zigzagging red lines. As he stares into them,
he begins to believe he is staring out of those eyes,
looking down at a thin blond boy on his front steps.
Then he lifts his head and still through the man's eyes
he sees the softness of late afternoon light on the street
where the man has spent his entire life, sees the green
of summer, white Victorian houses as through a white fog
so they shimmer and flicker before him. Looking past
the houses, past the first fields, he sees the reddening
sky of sunset, sees the land rushing west as if it wanted
to smash itself as completely as a cup thrown to the floor,
violently pursuing the sky with great spirals of red wind.

Abruptly the boy steps back. When he looks again into
the man's eyes, they appear bottomless and sad; and he
wants to touch his arm, say he's sorry about his mother,
sorry he's crazy, sorry he lets urine run down his leg
and wears a dress. Instead, he gives him his paper
and leaves. As he raises his bike, he looks out toward
red sky and darkening earth, and they seem poised
like two animals that have always hated each other,
each fiercely wanting to tear out the other's throat:
black dog, red dog—now more despairing, more resolved.

Frenchie

I was eating a chicken sandwich with mayonnaise
and reading about Russia when Frenchie stumbled
into the restaurant for a free cup of coffee.
He was drunk, but not too drunk to speak. Around me
blue-haired ladies nibbled Sunday dinners along with
other respectable types: bank clerk and plumber.
When he saw me, Frenchie asked how I was doing,
even though he has disliked me ever since I
kept him from hitting an old man with his crutch.
Frenchie needs a crutch because of the night he
dared the cop in the cruiser to drive over his foot.

Frenchie stood swaying at the front of the restaurant,
glaring at the blue-haired ladies who tried not to notice.
His face looks like a track team once sprinted across it.
In my book, the wife of the Russian poet was saying:
What will our grandchildren make of it if we all
leave the scene in silence? It was then Frenchie
decided to throw his cup to the floor and announce
he was going to die. Fragments of cup scattered around
my seat. Frenchie shouted: I'm sick and going to die and
no one cares. We all ate very quietly, as if listening
to the pop-pop of our taste buds self-destructing.

The waitress touched his arm. Oh, Frenchie, she said;
as if he wouldn't die; as if we would, but he wouldn't.
Don't give me that, he said. He was crying now. We each
pretended not to listen and I stared hard at my book,
but I thought we all had begun to imagine our own last
moments, as if Frenchie had put us in little theaters and
there on a stage the curtains were being noisily raised
and the elderly ladies, bank clerk, plumber, waitress

and myself—we all saw our funerals enacted before us: one
with a son come from Dallas, another with a sad Irish setter:
heaps of flowers, buckets of tears and an organ playing Bach.

But it wasn't so funny, because here we were on a Sunday
afternoon and I was concentrating on my chicken sandwich
and book where the woman was saying: What we wouldn't
have given for ordinary heartbreaks. And all of us
were trying to consume our small pleasures or at least
diversions, and I bet some of these ladies think too much
about death anyway, and here's Frenchie shouting I'm going
to die which takes the joy out of the meatloaf and mashed
potatoes. As for Frenchie, he's pure spite. I've seen him
hit little kids and he stands outside of bars making faces
at people through the glass and giving them the finger;

and just because the waitress was kind enough to offer him
a free cup of coffee he decided to remind us of the death
lurking in our future. So when he shouted that he's going
to die, I wanted to say: Sure, Frenchie, and can you do it
in the next few minutes? Let me help you find a truck,
walk you out to the end of the dock. Hey, I know a man
who's got a rabid dog. But maybe I was supposed to be
nice to him, take him home to meet my wife and kid,
let my wife cook him up some beans and franks, let him
fool around with my kid, wear my shirts and sweaters,
let him pat the cat. Hell, he'd probably eat the cat.

So none of that took place. Instead he stood there
shouting and his clothes were torn and he had vomit
on his shirt, and sure he would have liked someone
to give him ten bucks or a new life, but what he mostly
wanted was to grab us by our stomachs, our Sunday
dinners, yank us from our self-complacency and turn us
into witnesses, even though I had no wish to be a witness.
He wanted to make us take notice and say: Yes, you're

going to die, we're all going to die and that's too bad
and that's what sticks us in the same lousy boat
and no book or chicken sandwich will make it go away.

Maybe we should have stood up, confessed our mortality,
then crossed the street to the hardware that's open each
Sunday afternoon or wandered up to Barbara's Lunch or
the McDonald's out on the state highway. Maybe we ought
to have told everyone we met we were going to die and they
were going to die, until half the town is wandering around
tapping the other half on the shoulder, saying: Hey,
guess what? Then shake their hands and kiss them goodbye.
Maybe that would have been best, because in the restaurant
we all played dumb and nobody did a damn thing except
the waitress who said: Come on, Frenchie, you better go now.

As for me, I finished my sandwich, closed my book, pushed
past Frenchie and left, hoping to miss the tantrums,
the cops, the broken glass. But in the next few months,
I kept noticing Frenchie around town and he still
hadn't died, although twice I saw him being tossed
into the back of a cop car. Then this morning I see him
again as I'm driving through town, and it's a bright
blue morning at the beginning of March, and Frenchie
and a buddy are sunning themselves out in front of
the U-Ota-Bowl Alleys, and they're passing a bottle,
slapping their knees and having a high old time.

From this I guess Frenchie has forgotten he is
going to die, and I want to hang a U-turn, pull up
in front with my brand-new unpaid-for Volkswagen,
get out wearing my fashionable corduroys, down jacket
and expensive boots. Then I want to grab Frenchie
by the ears, kiss him smack on his vomit mouth,
sit down, drink a little Old Duke Red, tell a few
spiteful jokes, slap my knee and remind him that I'm

his witness, because even though he has forgotten
he's going to die, I haven't and what's more I'm
going to die too, as is his buddy, but what the hell.

In fact, maybe I should give him the car and down jacket,
not from guilt or that I've had better luck, but because
we're both going down the same slide. But who am I kidding?
I neither stopped the car nor waved, but drove straight to
my office with its books, papers and other shields against
the darkness, and after wasting time and making coffee and
staring out the window, I at last saw no hope for it and I
wrote down these words not because I saw myself in his eyes,
but from nothing more complicated than embarrassment.
The only way out of this life is to take him with me:
the left hand can't pretend it doesn't know the right.

The Great Doubters
of History

The woman who kicked out the back window
of the police cruiser sits chain-smoking and
drinking at a table by the dance floor.
Watching from a barstool, you doubt she
weighs over a hundred pounds. She is gaunt,
bony and resembles a fierce pygmy
warrior. One time she ripped off her clothes
in the parking lot, defied police to touch her.
Another time she pursued a patrolman
down the street, then kicked him in the balls.
Maybe she's twenty. Here in the bar she
seems jittery, can't hold her liquor, people
tell you, which is probably true, but you also
respect someone who knows she has nothing
to lose. You too have nothing to lose but spend
much of your time telling yourself you do.
In fact, it seems the point of society is to
make people think they have something to lose
until a man goes through life as nervously
as if he were carrying a teetery
stack of plates up a dark flight of stairs.

When the woman who kicked out the window
of the cop car dances, she shrugs her shoulders
and stamps her feet very fast as if she
weren't dancing but stamping on a multitude
of grievances. Mostly she dances by
herself because few men will ask her. You
nearly ask her, then change your mind, telling
yourself you are shy; but really you fear
that you too are something she can easily

let go, fear she'll see through your equivocations,
realize you think you have something to lose
and simply guffaw. Why dance with her at all?
Perhaps you think she might instruct you how
to shrug aside the trappings of your life,
because in her life nothing's there for keeps,
or so it seems, and you wish you had that
freedom from the things you own, but you don't
so at last you give it up and go home.
It's a clear spring night. In the parking lot,
two cops lean against their cruiser, staring
at the sky and idly waiting for trouble.

Are these the bad guys? Walking to your car,
you think of the fabric of value that surrounds you
as like the night itself, as if you could
poke your finger through it, as if the spots
of light you call stars were the places where
the great doubters of history had jabbed their thumbs.
The younger cop nods hello. You wonder
if they are waiting for the fierce woman
and if you should protect her, remove your
clothes and shout: Take me, take me. But you're not
the one they want in jail. You may have doubts,
but none to break the law for. As you drive home
beside the ocean, the moonpath follows you
on the water like a long finger of light.
Blame me, you say, go ahead, blame me.
Tomorrow you'll buy something you think you need,
ditto the next day, ditto the day after that.
Once home, you close and lock yourself inside,
as if you were both guard and prisoner—
prisoner with a question mark in your future
and no days off for your best behavior.

Kentucky Derby Day,
Belfast, Maine

When I was twelve, I happened to guess the winning horse
of the Kentucky Derby. It was on the sixth-grade
field trip to the Henry Ford Museum where we learned
that plain common sense is the key to the moral dominance
of the United States. The man on the car radio discussed
the horses and when he came to the name Dark Star, I said,
That's the horse for me. I mean, it seemed clear that any
horse named Dark Star *had* to win; and when Dark Star won,
I said, Sure—because in sixth grade life was like that.
My teacher said, Hey, you could have won a bundle.
I thought, What could be more simple? From that event
I date my readiness to be stupid about racehorses.

So on this May 2nd twenty-eight years later I shut down
my typewriter at five o'clock and hurry across to
Barbara's Lunch to watch the 107th running of the Derby.
It's been a lousy day and instead of writing or reading or
cleaning up my desk, I keep brooding that my marriage
is breaking apart, that my life seems aimed at a ditch,
is clearly out of control, and in the ornate bar mirror
I see my hair standing up in attitudes of bewilderment.
The restaurant is closed, TV dark and bar empty except for
the bartender, who's barely twenty and just learning to mix
cocktails, and a table of five people from the chicken plant
who I bet have been drinking beer and shots since breakfast.

Two of them are fast fat girls in tight shorts and loose
blouses and one wears a dog collar. Then there's a boy
as thin as a razor who has snipped off the sleeves of
his jean jacket and has homemade tattoos on his biceps
and bare shoulders. Another is a chain-smoking old man

destined, I'm sure, to die of cancer. And lastly
there is Leo, who resembles an aging country-western
singer, with a chin like a brick and thinning brown hair
swept back to look like Johnny Cash. The girl with
the dog collar strokes Leo's hand and tells the boy:
We love each other, we fight, but we love each other.
The boy nods. He may be no Apollo but he knows about love.

But this is Derby Day: twenty-one eager horses
and I'm told Tap Shoes is the horse to beat so I
call over the bartender and say, Hey, turn on the TV
and let's watch the Derby. He says, What's the Derby?
And I say, The Kentucky Derby. And he says, I never
heard of it. But he's a nice kid so he flicks on the TV
and there's Churchill Downs and thousands of flowers and
happy fans. Jesus, says the kid, look at all those people.
It's the Derby, I say: See, there's Muhammad Ali.
Who's that? says the kid. You know, I say, the great boxer.
Hey, says the kid, those horses going to pull little carts?
Not today, I say. Too bad, says the kid, I like the carts.

On the TV the announcer is predicting how the race
will be run and famous people are asked their opinions.
I wait for a twinkle in my brain but nothing happens. Still,
it's all so exciting I want to talk to someone about it—
say how making a bet is like falling in love or that
the horses and jockeys look like centaurs before the rape
of whoever—but the bartender is learning to make a Pink Lady,
while the five chicken processors are deep in their sadness.
The girl with the collar puts her hand on the boy's shoulder
and says, He needs me, Joey, I don't care if he hits me,
he wouldn't hit me if he didn't need to do it. And Leo says,
Listen, I'm no good. She thinks I'm good but I'm a pig.

The light from the door throws their shadows on the wall.
I think how defeated their lives are and wonder why

the girl wears a dog collar and what Leo must do
to mistreat her, if the old man will really die of cancer
and why the boy sticks holes in his arms to make dumb
tattoos with the name Jesse and little stars and crosses,
how he will die with that sentimental doodling still
on his body, having spent his life as a poor man's
advertisement for unrequited love. In no time I start
thinking of my own life with its insoluble problems—
how I can't afford health insurance and my parents
constantly fret and that my marriage is falling apart.

But on the TV they're getting ready for the run for
the roses—one hundred and forty thousand happy fans.
Maybe Bold Ego, I tell myself. Maybe Cure the Blues
or Proud Appeal. Maybe Top Avenger or Mythical Ruler.
What noble names. They all deserve to win. The bartender
looks up from his little red guide. I like gray horses best,
he says, it makes them look sad. Now they're in the gate.
The TV's by the jukebox and the flashing lights become all
the flowers at Churchill Downs. Then the bell and they're off.
Right away the horses string out rounding the first turn as
the favorites take an early lead. But oh-oh here comes the girl
with the dog collar with about five bucks for the jukebox.

Hold up, I tell her, this is a big race and it's almost over.
She's indifferent but polite so she waits. What's your horse?
she asks. Maybe Bold Ego, I say, unable to see him. I love
those country songs, says the girl. She stands beside me
and when I look down, I find I can look down her blouse.
But on the TV terrible things are happening: all the heroic
names are falling behind and coming up fast at the finish
is Pleasant Colony, while the number two horse, Woodchopper,
pays over twenty dollars and I'll bet they never announced
his name, because I spent half the damn winter chopping wood
and if I'd put a thousand on Woodchopper or even a hundred,
then right now I'd be winging my way south to better times.
*

Troy has fallen, I tell the girl, play those country songs.
She puts a hand on my arm. It's a crazy world, she says.
And I say, What's a smart girl like you doing here
in Barbara's Lunch? Why, she says, we're just waiting
for Big John to get us out of here. Aren't we all, I say.
The girl feeds her five bucks into the slot and goes back
to Leo, drapes herself over his shoulder as the jukebox
begins to pound out Take These Chains From My Heart,
which drowns out the TV where Pleasant Colony and jockey
Jorge Velasquez and trainer John Campo and the owner
Thomas Mellon Evans accept the quarter-of-a-million-
dollar purse and their corner on the world's happiness.

As I watch the horseshoe of roses being lowered onto
Pleasant Colony's neck, I think of my life and wonder
how to cope with my marriage coming down to certain divorce
and a son who will be the subject of long-distance calls
and for whom I'll be an occasional visitor. Is he taller?
I will ask. Is he doing well in school? And I will remember
kissing the soft part of his neck, the velvet indentation by
his collarbone, how I would nuzzle it and he would giggle.
On the TV the winners keep mouthing their thanks to the world
as the jukebox plays songs of infidelity and rejected love
and the girl with the dog collar keeps glancing at the door,
waiting for Big John who is a phenomenon I have no faith in.

But dammit all, I'm wrong. Just when I think it's a joke
in comes this big fellow and the girl jumps to her feet.
It's Big John, she says. And Big John looks foolish and grins.
He's a fat man in a red T-shirt that doesn't reach
his waist so the roll of fat looks like a white snake
wrapped round his belly. But everybody's perking up
and the girls twitch their shoulders. Come on, shouts
the one with the dog collar, Big John's got his Winnebago.
So we troop out to the street where the fog's rolling in and
parked at the curb is a golden Winnebago with a huge stereo,

soft chairs and all the beer you can drink. So what if you
don't know horses? So what if your life's shot to hell?

Hey, I shout, can your fat god in his fat machine fix my life?
Happy days ahead, calls the girl, hanging from the back step.
But before I can decide to act, Big John hits the gas.
The gutters of Belfast are filled with the white feathers
of chickens trucked daily to the processing plant, and as
Big John takes off feathers are swept up in his wake like
a taste of hot times. The Winnebago disappears into the fog,
like some wingéd Pegasus, I think, or Trojan Horse cruising
the coastline for holiday villages to pillage and burn.
In any case, it's gone and on the dead streets of Belfast
I find myself stuck without wonderful racehorse, joke
or sad life with which to divert myself by watching.

Where are the tricks to help me through the day? It's here
I must take my first step but I'm torn between Dark Star,
the Winnebago life or finding my way home where my wife tries
to push me from her heart because I've told her she must.
Think of the wedding pictures and everybody laughing.
Think of all the contemptible ways to say goodbye.
And unable to move a foot, I turn this way and that:
Dark Star, Dark Star, where are the winners I was promised?
But I'm not dumb; I know you only win when you bet real money
and play for keeps. Instead, I stand in the street as feathers
drift over my shoulders. Like Icarus? I ask myself, hopefully.
No, just another damn fool who won't make up his mind.

Between Hamburg and
Buenos Aires

Yesterday I took the dying taxicab that is my body
and we went swimming. As I swam, I thought
how the distance a single spermatozoan
swims from the testicles to the world is exactly
comparable to the distance swum by one man
churning the waves between Hamburg and Buenos Aires
four hundred times. No wonder we were born dying.
As I swam, I wanted to say, Hey, wait, save yourself.
As if the distance a single spermatozoan swims
from testicles to the world were the distance I might swim
from birth to death, as if my death were the egg which
this poor swimmer will someday fertilize, making me
the proud father of so many pounds of dead meat.

But here it is Christmastime in Santiago, Chile,
and all the dying taxicabs are moving a little faster.
The sidewalks are jammed with salesmen who rotate each hour
so the newsboy gives way to the guy selling fruit
who is replaced by men selling scissors, chewing gum,
Santa Claus dolls, lottery tickets, until at night
they are replaced by a succession of prostitutes
each getting more peculiar as the night gets later
so the last one carries a clear plastic violin case
filled with water and a single barracuda, until she
of course is replaced as dawn breaks by the newsboy—
Good night, Gladys. See you, Jose. Let's
call a stop. Let's bring a halt to the whole mess.
I mean, here I am in the backseat of this taxicab
watching the world rush by and I happen to take a gander
at the driver's picture on the hack license stuck
to the dashboard and I say to myself—Looks familiar,
skull and crossbones, wears a black hood. Now I know
in a serious poem you're not supposed to say,

Feet, do your stuff; but that's exactly what happened,
except I can't get the door open and soon
I realize this taxicab is mine for the duration.
Hey, I'm not a sophisticated guy. I was lucky
to get my college degree. But wherever I look,
there's Death. He's the elevator jockey's nefarious
bargain basement, the guy on the bus who turns
his neck to rubber trying to memorize my paper,
the big-footed dancer who stamps on my feet.
I tell you, I need a vacation; I need to forget.
I want to buy some bananas and go to the beach.
Say your uncle dies, and his wife and ten kids
move into your studio apartment. That's what Death is.
Say someone tosses you an open can of molasses
and everything you touch gets nasty. That's what Death is.
Say your bicycle's stuck on a treadmill and you keep
peddling faster because you think you see San Francisco
looming up ahead, but it's just the picture they put on
life's big screen to amuse you. That's what Death is.

But hold steady. This is only what happened yesterday
and basically yesterday was a pretty good day. I got up.
The sun was shining. I went swimming at the Y,
then walked back through Santiago wondering at
the oddness of Christmas in midsummer.
But the fact that people were pretty desperate
didn't bother me much or that every block had about
six beggars, six people playing fiddles and accordions
so badly you had to pay them to stop, plus another
dozen people selling trash from Taiwan, not including
the junk in the stores, so that every blessed moment
was measured by buying, selling and money changing hands.
But these were minor pimples on the living flesh
of my imagination because yesterday Death was no more
than a rider on a distant hilltop. And I remember
how cheerful I was yesterday, how many friends I had,
how much we ate and drank and how many jokes we told.

But today is another matter. Today it is cloudy.
I have quarreled with half my friends and the other half
have gone dancing without me. Even the mountains
have disappeared. And although it never rains in Santiago
in the summer, today it is raining and gray drops
spatter on the palm leaves. And I begin to realize
what was really wrong with yesterday. It is not until
the clarity of today do I see how futile it had been
to get out of bed, that intead of being far away
my Death had stayed as close as a sock to a foot.
So I put on some music to make myself feel better.
Dance, I say, strap on your wooden legs and dance.
But the men selling propane drive back and forth
hammering on metal tanks with metal sticks, then a baby
starts crying, then a car hits its brakes and the music
is overwhelmed the way a wave can overwhelm a rock.

So now my Death again appears before me and he has
changed his shirt and combed his hair and I think—
He doesn't look so bad. Who cares if his eyes are
too close together? So what if he has a weak chin?
He offers me his arm and we limp down the street.
I've been unhappy, I tell him, I've suffered great
disappointments. He pats my shoulder and I think I see
a tear glisten in the corner of his eye. You've been
much maligned, I say. He sighs and now I am certain
I see real tears and soon they are falling thick and fast.
You may not believe this but soon I am up to my knees
in salt water and it keeps getting deeper. First I start
to dog-paddle, then I begin my natural freestyle stroke.
This isn't so bad, I think, I can get used to this.
You ask how I could swim with a dying taxicab?
Once in the water it became a dying speedboat, rowboat,
tugboat, sailboat, kayak, dying canoe. What good fortune
to paddle forward on the sympathetic tears of Death himself,
which is how days now pass on the Hamburg–Buenos Aires
    Express.

Night Swimmer

Lifting his arms, the man half swims,
half thrashes his way to the dark shore
where he shakes himself, then threads a path
between the rocks to the first trees
where his horse is tied. Behind him
he has left two dead children whom he
found sleeping on cool summer sheets.
He had swum to the island to kill them
and, having finished his work, he unties
his horse and leads it quietly to the road.
Meanwhile, the father, who imagines his two sons
asleep in bed, stands at the other end
of the island, looking out over the lake.
High to his left hangs a half moon,
while near it is the constellation Orion.
The father thinks how his friends far off
in his own country see the same sky,
the same constellations, and it strikes him
that the three stars of Orion's belt
hang over his country like a finger.
Once more he begins his old argument
that for too long he has hidden himself
from the life of his homeland, that he must
return and help put his country in order.
Glancing back at his house, he sees a light
in the attic which then moves down the stairs,
and he guesses that a servant has gone
to cover the children. It is a square
white house and through the French windows
of his study, he sees the gray cat sleeping
on the papers on his desk. The night is windy
and the moon glimmers on rough water.
From the mainland, he hears the faint

clatter of hoofbeats and he wonders
what kind of person would be riding
so late and so far from home. Again
he thinks of the road to his own country
so that his desire to return and his fear
of defeat sway back and forth as he
considers the dangers and chances of success,
until he decides at last that he must
give up his exile, that it's not too late.
He thinks that once joined with his friends
they will destroy their enemies whose
only strength lies in their separation.
He looks back at his house where he hears
people shouting and calling his name
and so completely is he wrapped up
in his thoughts of returning that it seems
the servants have guessed his intentions
and are dragging the trunks down from the attic.
Across the lawn one of the servants
runs toward him, an old man whose white hair
and nightshirt flutter in the wind.
Eagerly the father hurries to greet him
and he doesn't notice how the servant
is crying, how his arms are outstretched.
Instead, he calls out they are leaving,
and in his mind is a confused memory
of cafés and wide boulevards, of sitting
with his friends on spring evenings, arguing
and feeling indignant about the world
in those days before his children were born
when he had only his own good name to lose.

Chinese Vase

Seats of red velvet as dark as a bloodstain,
I stand back in the wings to watch the stage
where a bear on a unicycle rides circles
around a boy dressed as a clown who juggles
two flaming torches. But the audience is bored
and the noise of people stirring and whispering
grows louder. The boy notices me watching

and I nod. In a moment, the act closes
to perfunctory applause. Someone praises me
on the performance. Should I tell him he lies
or let him know that I lie by thanking him?
Quickly, I see to the packing of costumes,
hoping to avoid the manager, but he stops me
at the door, then grins into my face

before letting me go. That afternoon
I had been waiting for him in his office.
When he arrived, I was standing over
the fragments of a small Chinese vase. I
explained it was an accident, that I hadn't
even touched it. On the contrary, he said,
you broke it because it was beautiful.

Much later I stare from the train window
as the landscape unrolls under a full moon.
I try to imagine men and women asleep
in those cottages, the smell of their bodies,
their legs entwined together, but the landscape
looks like a scene painted on canvas and propped
at the rear of the stage my train rushes across.

On the seat beside me, the boy is asleep,
covered by a red cloak. I decide to walk back

through the train. Here and there I see a man
smoking and staring from a window but most
of the compartments are dark. The bear's cage
is back in the baggage car and when he sees me,
he grunts and pushes his nose between the bars.

I search my pockets for something to give him
but they are empty. Scratching his snout,
I think of the years spent with this animal,
crisscrossing the country so people can
watch him dance. Taking a key, I unlock
the cage and let the bear out into the car.
The bear lowers his muzzle into my hand.

I kneel down and feel certain that my face
resembles his face—questioning and stupid.
The side door of the car is partly open
and I look out at the night sky. In the distance,
the lights of a town join together into one
great cluster of light and I think, that is youth
seen from the solitary darkness of age—

a place where audiences cheer and the bears
are all young. The door rattles beneath my hand
and I tell myself that I must go back, must
return the bear to his cage, but like a child
allowed to stay up for some special event
I beg myself for just another minute
as the lights seem to coalesce into memory.

There is my marriage and the birth of my son.
There is a woman's face, her hair held back
by a black ribbon. I reach out to touch
the dead white cheek. Her face rushes toward me
as the moon breaks from behind cloud. Light, light
speckles the landscape like pieces of Chinese vase.
I reach out my hand and it seems I am flying.

That I Have Lied and
Spoken Foolishly

That I have lied and spoken foolishly,
that I have betrayed myself, been cruel
to those around me—such thoughts weigh upon me

this summer morning as I watch a red sun
balance on the farthest line of ocean
as if ready to sink or simply stay there

like a spiteful eye that always knows better,
until I need to tell myself it will rise,
that it always rises. On the porch at my feet

my small son, who chose this morning to get up
at five, builds a tower with four blocks, watches
it fall, builds it, watches it fall again.

Around me is the life I have willed for myself:
half-painted house, garden, eight cords of wood
to be cut and stacked for the coming winter.

Last night in another quarrel, you raised
your fist in frustration or disbelief
and I swung out, striking you in the chest,

knocking you back. As you fell, your head
banged against a chair so you cried out
and writhed half-naked on the kitchen floor,

pressing your hands to your face and twisting
like a snake partly crushed by a car. As I
stood in the doorway, I said you deserved it,
*

as if you were an animal in need of punishment
and not the beautiful woman who shares my bed.
My wife, my wife, what poor end have we come to?

Victrola

Tedium of Sunday afternoons: tedium of sprawling
on the parlor floor, drawing and wrangling
with my cousin over what looked most like writing—
his angular jabs or my squiggles; tedium
of picture books, of shaking the glass snowstorm
for the thousandth time, of listening to adults
discuss who was sick or who had a new car;
tedium of clocks stuck between three and three-
thirty, no matter how many pages turned, clock ticks
counted, breaths taken and held; tedium of waiting
for the world of benign law to fall asleep
so we could escape into the huge house filled
with breakable objects, dogs too proper to be teased
and antimacassars, antimacassars everywhere—
this was the well-scrubbed universe, home of
the straight line and china bowl, temple of orderly
devotion and hard peppermint candies, smell of
furniture polish and applesauce cooking on the stove.

Sometimes we escaped as far as the ramshackle barn
with my great grandfather's buggies, the fastest
in Lewis County; and the piles of blankets,
leather harness, pikes, axes and sawblades
from my grandfather's lumber camps—musty smell
of wool, straw and leather; labyrinth in a twilight
of mattresses stacked to the ceiling, creaking
bedsprings, barrels of nails, coils of oiled rope.
Sometimes we explored the attic of the house, a high
square room with a swing in the middle, an empty
birdcage, a dressmaker's dummy with a black
floor-length dress. My cousin and I poked through
trunks of old clothes, put on blue straw hats
with beaded veils, tried to climb the rope
to the trapdoor in the roof, tried to imagine

the children who kept diaries with entries like—
Today I went sledding and was good all day;
studied a picture of our beautiful great aunt
who died at age twelve from hitting her head
on a branch; how my cousin thought he loved her,
and how her death made us hate the world.

In the playroom downstairs was a wind-up Victrola.
I'd wind and wind, then watch an old cracked record
begin its delirious rush as the needle and bulky
silver arm rode it like a cowboy at a matinee.
Open the little doors and from far away those
scratchy foxtrots filled the room while my cousin
and I swirled in separate circles. That was 1946—
the war just over and returning uncles still
in naval uniforms. Those foxtrots seemed to bind it
all together, seemed to activate the clothes and
memories of the attic, the murky libido of the barn,
and in their rush and swirl described that benign
order which we assumed would continue forever—
my cousin and I already smoking and planning
to be basketball stars or simply travel and
have a horse and perhaps play basketball as well.

Maybe it lasted another summer. Then one aunt died
and the other decided to sell everything and move
to an apartment. Shortly before the auction,
my cousin and I broke into the house, wandered
its twenty rooms. I remember the surprise of
discovering how the permanent could be so easily
pushed aside—dirt on the floor, broken dishes,
books in a heap, the delicate filigree bowls
stacked high in liquor boxes. Then came
the auction itself—a bright, midsummer morning,
rows of chairs on the grass facing the front porch,
the big lawn bordered with cars come all the way
from Buffalo. Bit by bit the house was sold
from the front steps as strangers fingered

the antimacassars and made their trifling bids.
To think that such a world could be so simply
turned to money, so quickly disposed of with
fast talk, wisecracks and the signing of a name—
my cousin and I tried to disrupt the auction
with false bids shouted from the back row,
until we were caught, threatened with expulsion.
So we sat quietly and watched the breakup
of all those Sunday afternoons. Toward the end,
they dragged out the Victrola. The auctioneer
played part of a silly song. The buyer from
New York yawned and bought a Coke, and some
local joker took home the Victrola for two bucks.

All that happened years ago. My cousin is dead.
The house has been sold at least six more times.
Even the small town where we went each summer
has become just a place that people move away from.
But recently in the classroom of a school where
I was teaching was a Victrola like the one
auctioned from my great aunt's front steps.
Someone was trying to work it but didn't know how.
But I knew how, knew every lever, knew where
the records were kept and seconds later a squawky
tenor voice was piping out Goodnight Sweetheart
as everybody laughed. It was winter and snowing.
From the window, I watched how the bare trees seemed
caught in the act of poking and jabbing each other.
The blowing snow resembled layers of sheer curtains
and to look at the hills through their white shadow
was like the process of memory. I tried to focus
on how the snow swirled around the distant trees
and it seemed that in their faraway motion
I could see figures passing back and forth between
their boughs, but not clearly, not so they ever became
recognizable as people. And who would they have been?
I thought of how deep the snow lay and what it concealed—
all that lay sleeping, all that was dead or forgotten.

Dead Baby

(Helen Johnston, 1882–1968)

My great aunt had a story she often repeated
when she was old and losing her memory
about driving out to take care of a sick baby.
She was a nurse and this was one of her first cases
so it must have been around the turn of the century.
The baby's mother lived in a big house on Leyden Hill.
It was winter and my aunt had to go in the sleigh.
She was a slender woman, not much over five feet,
and easily frightened of her world going out of control
and by what she called rough men. She never married.
The house was a square, three-story Victorian house
and when my aunt got there she discovered the baby
dead in its crib, and the mother—apparently alone
in the house—exhausted and hysterical. By then
it was dark, and my aunt sent the woman to bed,
saying she would sit with the dead child. Eventually,
she fell asleep only to be waked late at night by
the bump and scrape of someone limping across the floor.
By the light of the candle, she saw a blind man
stumbling toward her and she leapt from her chair.
Here my aunt would often stop as if having reached
the conclusion. Then she would look uncertain
and ask if I'd ever heard the story she had told
at the banquet honoring her fifty years of nursing;
at which point, she would begin the whole story again—
the news of the sick baby, the sleigh, the discovery
of its death, the blind man stumbling through the dark.
But each time she told it she would add new details,
so when the man approached with his arms outstretched
my aunt saw that both arms had been cut off at the wrist,
that he was feeling his way forward with the two stumps.
Then, in another version, she saw that around one stump
the man had wrapped a rosary of jet-black beads.

My aunt said she flattened herself against the wall,
believing the blind man was after her, but then
he continued past her and made his way to the crib,
where he bent over and cried, fumbling his arms
against the dead baby, trying to embrace it, and how
he was unable to lift it, how it kept falling back.
After an hour, he stumbled away in the dark, still
crying and bumping together the ruins of his arms.
In the morning, my aunt learned the man was a brother
who had been wounded in the Civil War, or in another
retelling she said he had been hurt in a train accident,
but perhaps the accident had taken place during the war.
My aunt would sit in her small room in a home for
the elderly, a gray stone building with thick walls,
supposedly the oldest house in Martinsburg, and say how
she wanted to go home and how unfair it all was.
Piled on a tray in front of her were stacks of cards
from relatives, neighbors, friends and old co-workers,
and as she talked she constantly picked through them
as if rereading the script of her life, as if
without these reminders it would all slip away and
she would sit there blankly, like a darkened lamp.
So each day she read out the names, retold her stories
and complained she was well enough to go home,
which she never did because she died in that room,
in that home for the elderly which later went broke
and is now a high-priced restaurant for skiers
up from New York City. And I try to think of those
immaculate skiers eating prime rib in the room
where my aunt fumbled with her memory and repeated
her stories, always returning to the story of the baby,
as if the baby signified the remnants of her life,
by then mostly forgotten, but which she was still
trying to reclaim and embrace, in the way the blind
veteran with his hands sliced off at the wrist
had again and again tried to lift the baby from its crib
only to fail and feel it slip and fall away.

Jason at Eighty

After forty years of being kicked around Greece,
Jason returned to the Isthmus of Corinth
where the *Argo* had been beached: golden ship
with fifty oars made with seasoned timber
from Mount Pelion. Jason sat down by the ship
and took from his pouch a small rag which he
unwrapped to reveal a minuscule sliver of vanity,
like a small lump of coal or crystal knife
that flickered in the sunlight. Staring into it,
Jason considered his past glories, by then so far
in the past he had to hear them sung about
before he could say, Yes, that's it, that's
how it happened. But slowly he recalled the yoking
of the fire-breathing bulls, sowing the field
with dragon's teeth, the theft of the golden fleece
as he chased one shining temptation after another.
Think of the mistakes that young man made. Handsome,
of good family, educated in the best schools,
he had never anticipated failure. Therefore,
when his devious uncle sent him to fetch the ram's
fleece from Colchis nothing had seemed easier.
He hired himself a crew, bought the best boat
and despite mistake after stupid mistake he always
squeaked through, depending on those with more brains
to save him from the jams in which he found himself,
whether Hercules, Orpheus or Medea, that daughter
of Colchis whose other most famous resident was Stalin.

In reward, Jason received the kingdom of Corinth,
no matter that he was married to a witch, had
broken oaths and left behind a trail of pillage
which, if he hadn't committed, he had certainly
condoned, had slept with every woman he could catch

and thought her well repaid if she could bear his brat.
Jason was the kind of man who if he fell from a window
would land in a passing wagon of hay; the soldier
whose breast pocket Bible stops the fatal bullet.
After a youth of self-indulgence, good luck and
cheering crowds, he must have felt badly tricked
when his world collapsed just because he cheated
on Medea and broke his trust with the gods.
How could he have thought that was the line
not to be crossed—he, who had crossed so many?
But in no time his new girl friend went up in smoke,
his sons were slaughtered and Jason found himself
stripped of his crown and bustled from Corinth without
so much as a toothbrush, reference or casual goodbye.
The gates slammed shut, guards on the walls tossed down
a few rocks and Jason wound up on the outside forever—
left to fend for himself, the one thing he could not do.
For the next forty years he sought out old cronies
who refused even to see him. He lived as an outcast,
whose only treasure was that tiny sliver of vanity
which he carried with him like a lump of coal or
crystal knife with which to gouge and torment himself.

But eventually he returned to the Isthmus of Corinth
and as Jason crouched down within the shadow of the *Argo*,
scratching himself and muttering complaints,
he took out that smidgen of vanity and unwrapped it
and, oh, it was battered and barely gave off a shine
but as he peered into its corners it began to twinkle
and generate a light at last bright enough to blind him
to the bad parts—the betrayed promises and comrades
forsworn—and despite his eighty years and judgment
of the gods Jason believed he was still a hero and that
he who had been scorned should now scorn the world
by assuming his punishment and taking his own life.
And staring up at the *Argo* glittering in the late

afternoon sun, Jason grabbed a rope, knotted
a noose and flung it over the prow of the ship.
And it's this that makes him great, not the girls
and good times and flashing acts of bravado, but that
forty years of punishment had taught him zero,
that despite hardship and all the evidence
to the contrary, Jason still thought he could escape
the world's sentence by hurling his ego furiously
against it, like a rock through a plate-glass window.
But the world, here in the form of the *Argo* herself,
would have none of it, and as Jason cranked up his courage
to hang himself in a last gesture of self-assertion,
the *Argo* shuddered, rolled out of the sunlight, toppled
and crushed Jason, a puny figure standing in the sand.

Pacos

Eight people lean over a wall looking down
twenty feet to the shallow Mapocho River
where a man's body lies half-covered by water.

Behind the eight people are trees, the bronze
bust of an Argentine poet and the law school
of the University of Chile. The man in the river

wears a white shirt, dark pants and sprawls
as if sleeping while water riffles his hair.
This is a photograph from the coup or *golpe*,

meaning also hit or shock—just one death
from thirty thousand. Each day, nine years later,
I ride the bus past this place. When did his

family begin to worry? Now, in late summer,
the Mapocho is hardly a trickle, a narrow
sewer, where vegetable vendors throw their

spoiled tomatoes, where you sometimes see
a dead dog or broken shopping cart.
When this man was growing up, what plans

did his father have for him? At the corner
is where candy salesmen wait to clamber
aboard the buses to sell peanuts, mints,

chewing gum for ten pesos. What does it mean
to commit an irrevocable act, to kill
someone, to steal a thing you can't give back?
*

Four blocks away stands the American consulate,
four blocks in another direction is the house
of Pablo Neruda—both were close enough

to hear the shot that killed this man.
And how did he die? Was he a communist
or right wing spy shot by mistake? What

electric fillip in the cerebral cortex
justified the erasure of this man? Perhaps
he was a law student who thought he could

make it home after curfew, run the two or
three short blocks through the dark. After
a while, it becomes a joke to kill someone,

the ultimate comic act, the extreme slip
on the final banana. After a while, it's
the fun we all take part in. A policeman

saw him running, followed him with the sights
of his rifle and suddenly the young man
was doing somersaults. When did his friends

begin to miss him? Did he have a girl friend?
Did he have sisters and brothers? Some days I
walk back through Forrestal Park by the river—

watching the lovers sitting on park benches.
Every twenty feet there's another statue
of another famous man. Policemen or *pacos*

patrol the sidewalk two by two—*pacos* being
the rude name I break the law by using,
which originally meant a great leather bag
*

of water. How long did he lie in the river?
How long did he stay in the morgue before
his family found him? It would take at least

two policemen to lift him—one at the feet,
one at the shoulders—to heave him over the wall.
How they must have laughed at such a crazy splash.

Cuidadores de Autos

It seems like the world's most useless profession—
to guard and protect the already safe and secure,
to guide you out of your parking place as if
this were your first time behind the wheel; as if
without their help you would smash into one car,
then another or collapse and weep uncontrollably;
that without them to put your peso in the meter,
you would desperately fumble, accidentally fling it
down the grating of a sewer. There must be
a thousand of these men on the streets of Santiago
with their symbols of office—a dirty
orange rag and a gray cap. I even know one man
who is training his son in the profession:
a boy of about eight with a smaller cap and
smaller rag. The father complains how people
ignore him, force him to chase them all the way
to the stoplight for his *propina* which is why he
employs his little boy who is quick on his feet
and likes to run. But I remember one night
when we had dinner at a restaurant near the market.
We had not argued that day. You were happy
and your eyes crinkled at the corners in a way
that makes you even more beautiful. When we
left the restaurant, yours was the only car still
on the block, and nearby waited one of these men,
these caretakers of cars, but older than most
and with a gray cap that looked like something
had been chewing it. He followed us to the car and
with great ceremony directed you away from the curb
with his little orange rag, peered intently into
the dark for any trucks that might be traveling

fast with their lights off. The world was safe
and the innocent slept soundly in their beds.
You thanked him, gave him ten pesos and he
called you his little daughter which pleased
and embarrassed you. The moon was full that night
but the moon here is not the northern moon;
the face is another face. The right eye that
I have seen all my life is now the mouth,
and the mouth of the north is now the left eye—
a face with a high forehead, no chin to speak of,
a leering, stupid sort of face which presumes
to know, but knows nothing. As you slept,
I studied the freckles on your back until they
seemed part of a map—towns with no roads
between them. Here everything feels reversed.
The fig tree in the backyard was heavy with figs
and I kept hearing them fall: first a brief riffle
as one dropped through the leaves, then a plop
like a wet, wadded-up sock as it hit the tiles
of the patio where it would harden and spoil.
You lay dreaming of houses—solar houses and
earthquake-proof houses, a house on the beach
with sunlight flickering on the white walls,
filling the rooms like water. And where was I?
Sometimes I hear sirens during curfew, the high
squealing sirens of the motorcycles; and that night
there were gunshots and the sound of running.
A German newspaper claims that last month
twenty-one houses were raided in Santiago,
442 political arrests. We know nothing of it.
Later that night a jeep slammed on its brakes.
There was shouting, the sound of someone being beaten.
We hurried outside. A young man lay in the grass,
moaning and holding his head. He said he had been
at a party. There had been a girl. He wore new

expensive-looking yellow boots and pleaded with us
not to call the police. Soon we went back to bed.
Who will protect us from our protectors?
As I lay beside you I listened to the sound of
the man's boots walking slowly down the street,
becoming fainter until at last they were lost
and grew confused with the pounding of my heart.

What You Have Come
to Expect

The worn plush of the seat chafes your bare legs
as you shiver in the air-conditioned dark
watching a man embrace his wife at the edge
of their shadowy lawn. It is just past dusk
and behind them their house rises white and
symmetrical. Candles burn in each window,
while from the open door a blade of light jabs
down the gravel path to a fountain. In the doorway
wait two children dressed for sleep in white gowns.
The man touches his wife's cheek. Although
he must leave, he is frightened for her safety and
the safety of their children. At last he hurries
to where two horses stamp and whinny in harness.
Then, from your seat in the third row, you follow him
through battles and bloodshed and friends lost
until finally he returns home: rides up the lane
as dusk falls to discover all that remains of his house
is a single chimney rising from ashes and mounds of debris.
Where is his young wife? He stares out across
empty fields, the wreckage of stables and barns.
Where are the children who were the comfort of his life?

In a few minutes, you plunge into the brilliant light
of the afternoon sun. Across the street, you see your bike
propped against a wall with your dog waiting beside it.
The dog is so excited to see you she keeps leaping up,
licking your face, while you, still full of the movie,
full of its colors and music and lives sacrificed to some
heroic purpose, try to tell her about this unutterable
sadness you feel on a Saturday afternoon in July 1950.
Bicycling home, you keep questioning what happened

to the children, what happened to their father standing
by the burned wreckage of his house, and you wish
there were someone to explain this problem to, someone
to help you understand this sense of bereavement and loss:
you, who are too young even to regret the passage of time.
Next year your favorite aunt will die, then your
grandparents, one by one, then even your cousins.
You sit on the seat of your green bike with balloon tires
and watch your dog waiting up the street: a Bayeux
tapestry dog, brindle with thin legs and a greyhound chest,
a dog now no more than a speck of ash in the Michigan dirt.
From a distance of thirty years, you see yourself paused
at the intersection: a thin blond boy in khaki shorts;
see yourself push off into the afternoon sunlight,
clumsily entering your future the way a child urged on
by its frightened nurse might stumble into a plowed field
in the dead of night: half running, half pulled along.
Behind them: gunshots, flame and the crack of burning wood.
Far ahead: a black line of winter trees.

Now, after thirty years, the trees have come closer.
Glancing around you, you discover you are alone;
raising your hands to your face and beard, you find
you are no longer young, while the only fires
are in the fleck of stars above you, the only face
is the crude outline of the moon's: distant, as any family
you might have had; cold, in a way you have come to expect.

Art

It's almost an old joke: two Albanian cooks
murder a prostitute, cut up the body and stick
the various bits into five black garbage bags.
The torso is never found and the restaurant
goes broke. Except some little kid opens up
one of the bags, and you, as a newspaper reporter,
are sent out to see him, taking a photographer
along to get art, as your editor tells you.

The boy is ten and delivers papers. For a week,
he's been noticing these bags in an empty lot
and today he decided to check one out. You sit
in his parents' kitchen and he sits before you,
hands in his lap. He's quiet and dark-haired,
and his parents look at him as if he were a watch
they'd accidentally dropped from a second-
story window, then seen split open by a truck.

The parents are poor and their kitchen smells of all
the vegetables you've ever hated. The boy tells you
that when he tore open the bag and saw the arm, he
at first thought it was the leg of a deer. He speaks
hesitantly as if he were dragging the words themselves
from that bag: foul-skinned and unpronounceable, while
you think what a week of summer heat in a plastic bag
could do to a woman's arm to make it look like that.

A few days later the Albanians are picked up
in New York City speeding through Times Square
in an open convertible. In the trunk, police find
burglar tools and one hundred eight-by-ten glossy

photographs showing one of the Albanians posed
naked with a knife from one hundred different angles.
As the cop tells you over the phone, he was certain
that someplace someone wanted them for something.

The prostitute happened to be a girl from the suburbs:
a high school graduate with hardworking parents,
who hoped to become a certified public accountant.
Her friends said she was a nice girl, but quiet.
The Albanians claimed they never knew she was
a prostitute until she demanded money, at which point
they grew indignant. Actually, it was the girl's
former respectability the paper found important,

but for you the Albanians, the girl and her missing
torso are only the dark gossip of a darker world.
Instead, you are moved by the boy carefully telling you
he was certain he had come upon the leg of a deer,
but then he had seen the hand, the curled fingers,
and that darker world had smashed and broken through
the five doors of his senses, had snatched him up
to wear as a trinket around its own thick neck.

When you write the story of the murder, the detail
about the boy foolish enough to think he'd discovered
a source of free venison in the heart of Detroit
to feed him and his family forever comes out
as a phrase in the twelfth 'graph; and although they
run the kid's photo, they print it with the jump
at the back of the third section, and you wonder
why you bother writing anything down. Still, you

consider how your editor leafed through the pictures
on his paper- and telephone-littered desk and at
last chose the one of the boy uneasily touching

his own cheek with the tips of his fingers as if he
could feel the cheek of some different kid, the cheek
of a kid now strange to him; and your editor looked up
and said, Not bad; then waved to the picture editor,
calling, Hey Wolfie, there's good art coming.

Truth

It was a simple case of a girl needing a place to stay.
As for the man, he owned a four-room house in the suburbs
and decided to take on a boarder. He dealt drugs
as a hobby and had never met the girl until she
answered his ad. A day later some person or persons
unknown turned up and blew them both away
for drugs, money or revenge there was no way to figure
so your editor sent you out to look things over.

It was a yellow house set off in a ragged field,
and when you arrived police, sheriff and state police
were measuring, taking pictures, dusting for prints:
getting to the bottom of it, they said. The dead man
was twenty-five and had a record. If it weren't for the girl,
your editor said, it would merely be another
two-bit murder. She was an eighteen-year-old clerk
who'd never done anything important until now.

The dead man owned thirty cats and five dogs.
The cats kept prowling all over and when the cops
kicked them out one door, the cats came padding back
through another. The dead man had been painting the house
and had just finished painting the front room white. Whoever
killed them, took them into that room, then shot them
each four times. It was a small room and empty except
for a large red motorcycle, a Harley 1250.

The police set up lights in the white room and were
dusting for prints. You stood at the front door.
Every square inch of the floor was evenly covered
with the blood of the drug dealer and his boarder.
The red motorcycle rose up as if sculpted from

blood and light to represent the murder, while
with supreme delicacy the thirty cats one after
another tiptoed across the screaming red floor.

The police put on black rubbers and they too tiptoed
through the blood, pursuing the cats, but slowly, not
wanting to splash or slip. Out came one cat, in came
another until all over were trails of red pawprints.
The five dogs cowered in a heap. They knew trouble
when they saw it, although it didn't save them, for when
the truck came from the pound they were the first ones
tossed inside. A week later the police were still no

wiser about the murder, while the pound said the thirty
cats had been destroyed. Who'd want thirty adult cats?
As for the mystery, you kept thinking of the girl who must
have thought herself lucky to find a place in the country,
who was ready to go back to Walgreen's on Monday. Maybe
she liked cats, liked motorcycles, liked the way he was
fixing the place up. And you wonder when she realized
her mistake. As more weeks passed, you kept thinking of

the moment the truck from the pound pulled from the driveway,
when the cats, which had been quiet, began to yowl and
hurl themselves at the wire mesh, until the whole back
of the truck shook, and the cops looked up and you all
watched the cats as if they were howling at you, howling
at the dumb cops, dumb reporter, howling at the measuring
and note-taking. And you recalled too how the cops carried
the cats to the truck, trying to keep the blood-smeared feet

from touching their uniforms, until in memory it seemed
the cats themselves were being arrested, as if they knew
too much, as if their prints spelled out a story you could
never write: sentence after red sentence winding

through the house, describing the very instant when the girl at last understood, when her knowledge became as real as the red motorcycle rising up from the floor. At which point, someone's .38 blew her all over the fresh white paint.

Beauty

The father gets a bullet in the eye, killing him
instantly. His daughter raises an arm to say stop
and gets shot in the hand. He's a grocer from Baghdad
and at that time lots of Iraqis are moving to Detroit
to open small markets in the ghetto. In a month,
three have been murdered and since it is becoming
old news your editor says only to pick up a photo
unless you can find someone half decent to talk to.

Jammed into the living room are twenty men in black,
weeping, and thirty women wailing and pulling their hair—
something not prepared for by your Episcopal upbringing.
The grocer had already given the black junkie his money
and the junkie was already out the door when he fired,
for no apparent reason, the cops said. The other daughter,
who gives you the picture, has olive skin, great dark eyes
and is so beautiful you force yourself to stare only

at the passport photo in order not to offend her.
The photo shows a young man with a thin face cheerfully
expecting to make his fortune in the black ghetto.
As you listen to the girl, the wailing surrounds you
like bits of flying glass. It was a cousin who was shot
the week before, then a good friend two weeks before that.
Who can believe it? During the riots, he told people
to take what they needed, pay when they were able.

Although the girl has little to do with your story,
she is, in a sense, the entire story. She is young,
beautiful and her father has just been shot. As you
accept the picture, her mother grabs it, presses it

to her lips. The girl gently pries her mother's fingers
from the picture and returns it. Then her sister with
the wounded hand snatches the picture and you want to
unwrap the bandages, touch your fingers to the bullet hole.

Again the girl retrieves the picture, but before she
can give it back, a third woman in black grabs it,
begins kissing it and crushing it to her bosom. You think
of the unflappable photographers on the fourth floor
unfolding the picture and trying to erase the creases,
but when the picture appears in the paper it still bears
the wrinkles of the fat woman's heart, and you feel caught
between the picture-grabbing which is comic and the wailing

which is like an animal gnawing your stomach. The girl
touches your arm, asks if anything is wrong, and you say,
no, you only want to get out of there; and once back
at the paper you tell your editor of this room with fifty
screaming people, how they kept snatching the picture.
So he tells you about a kid getting drowned when he was
a reporter, but that's not the point, nor is the screaming,
nor the fact that none of this will appear in a news story

about an Iraqi grocer shot by a black drug addict,
and see, here is his picture as he looked when he first
came to our country eight years ago, so glad to get
out of Baghdad. What could be worse than Baghdad?
The point is in the sixteen-year-old daughter giving back
the picture, asking you to put it in your pocket, then
touching your arm, asking if you are all right and
would you like a glass of water? The point is she hardly

belongs to that room or any reality found in newspapers,
that she's one of the few reasons you get up in the morning,
pursue your life all day and why you soon quit the paper

to find her: beautiful Iraqi girl last seen surrounded by
wailing for the death of her father. For Christ's sake,
those fools at the paper thought you wanted to fuck her,
as if that's all you can do with something beautiful,
as if that's what it means to govern your life by it.